This book belongs to:

Note to parents and carers

Many children are now taught to read using the phonic approach. This means they are taught to look at the letters, say the sounds, and then blend them to make a word. So, for example, children blend **c/a/t** to make the word **cat**, and **sh/o/p** to make **shop**.

When children have completed their initial phonics learning, they are ready to apply it to reading real books. Ladybird's **Superhero Phonic Readers** are planned for this exciting stage.

Some words are hard to read using beginner phonics. These words are often known as 'tricky words'. Some of these occur frequently in the English language so it is useful for children to memorize them.

Have fun doing our Tricky Words Memory Quiz on page 30. This features the most useful tricky words from the story.

How to use Superhero Phonic Readers:

✴ Start at level one and gradually progress through the series. Each story is a little bit longer than the last and uses more grown-up vocabulary.

✴ Children will be able to read **Superhero Phonic Readers** for themselves. Let your child read to you, and share the excitement!

✴ If your child finds any words difficult, help him or her to work out the sounds in the word.

✴ Early readers can be concentrating so hard on the words that they sometimes don't fully grasp the overall meaning of what they read. The puzzle questions on pages 28 and 29 will help with this. Have fun talking about them together.

✴ There is a reward chart at the back of the book – young readers can fill this in and add stickers to it.

✴ The Ladybird website **www.ladybird.com** features a wealth of information about phonics and reading.

✴ Enjoy reading together!

Geraldine Taylor
Ladybird Educational Consultant

Educational Consultant: Geraldine Taylor

Phonics Consultant: Marj Newbury

A catalogue record for this book is available from the British Library

Published by Ladybird Books Ltd
80 Strand, London, WC2R 0RL
A Penguin Company

2 4 6 8 10 9 7 5 3 1
© LADYBIRD BOOKS LTD MMIX
LADYBIRD and the device of a Ladybird are trademarks of Ladybird Books Ltd

ISBN: 978-1-40930-253-7

Printed in Italy

Superhero Phonic Readers

Zain Zoom

written by Mandy Ross

illustrated by Ingela Peterson

This is Zain Zoom as a baby. He is very speedy.

And this is Zain Zoom as a boy. He is very, very speedy!

Zain Zoom is training to be a superhero.

"I need a superhero skill," says Zain. "I must be super speedy."

Zain runs and runs. He runs up hills.
He runs down hills. He runs in zigzags.

He runs in the sun.

He runs in the rain.

Soon, Zain can run faster than a car, or a train, or a plane!

Now, Zain is ready to be a speedy superhero.

"Miss Viper has got my dog!" says Mr Poodle.

Mr Poodle runs after Miss Viper, but he is too slow to catch up with her.

Miss Viper can run very fast,
but she is not super speedy like Zain.

Zain runs after her.

Miss Viper says, "I need to go faster."
She jumps into a car.

Zain Zoom runs after the car.
Do not do this at home, readers.

Miss Viper says, "I need to go faster."
She jumps from the car onto a train.

Zain Zoom chases the train.
Do NOT do this at home, readers.

Miss Viper says, "I need to go faster."
She jumps into a plane.

Zain Zoom runs after the plane.
NEVER do this at home, readers.

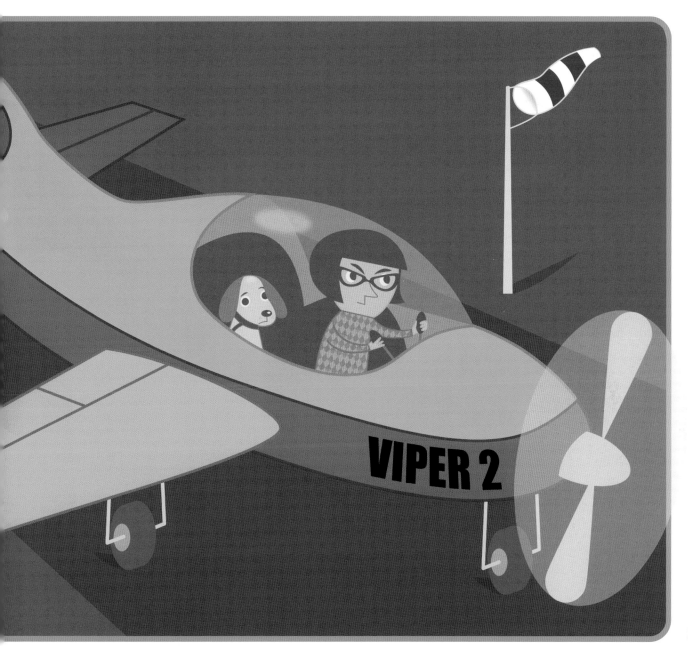

Zain Zoom catches up with the plane and turns the motor off. You CANNOT do this at home, readers.

Zain grabs Miss Viper and Pooch. What a superhero!

Pooch is happy to see Mr Poodle.
Mr Poodle is happy to see Pooch.

PC Plod is happy to see Miss Viper.
Miss Viper is not happy to see PC Plod…

And everybody is happy to see Zain Zoom.
"Happy to help," says Zain Zoom,
the super speedy superhero.

Superhero secret puzzles

⭐ What is Zain Zoom's super skill?

⭐ Who does Pooch belong to?

⭐ Who stole Pooch?

⭐ How did Zain Zoom stop the plane?

⭐ Are you super speedy?

Look at these pictures from the story and say the order they should go in.

A

B

C

D

Answer on page 30.

Tricky Words Memory Quiz

Can you remember these words from the story?

See if you can read them super-fast.

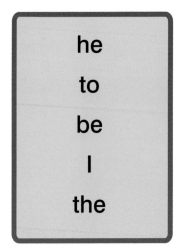

he
to
be
I
the

do
my
Mr
go
her

she
you
into
what

What else can you remember?

Can you put the book down and say what happens in the story?

The answer to the picture puzzle on page 29 is: D, A, C, B.

I'm a phonic
Superhero

I can read all of *Zain Zoom*.

I can read all the tricky words.

By _____

Date _____

level
2

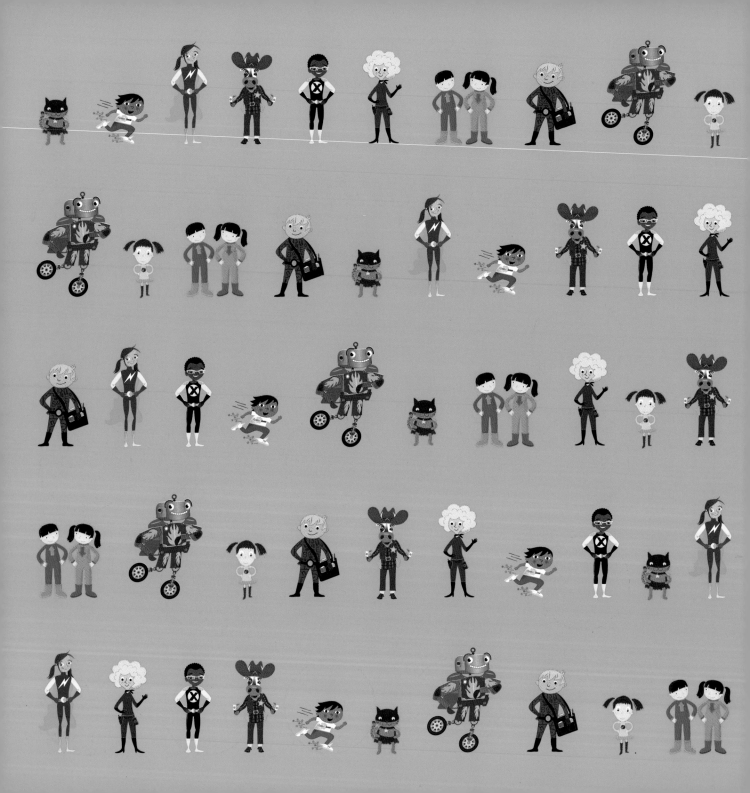

I did great work

Well done!

I can read tricky words

I'm a phonics reader

I'm a reading hero

Zain Zoom

Miss Viper

Zain Zoom

Miss Viper

Zain Zoom

Super Speedy

Super Speedy

Super Speedy

Super Speedy